Talking About Pianos

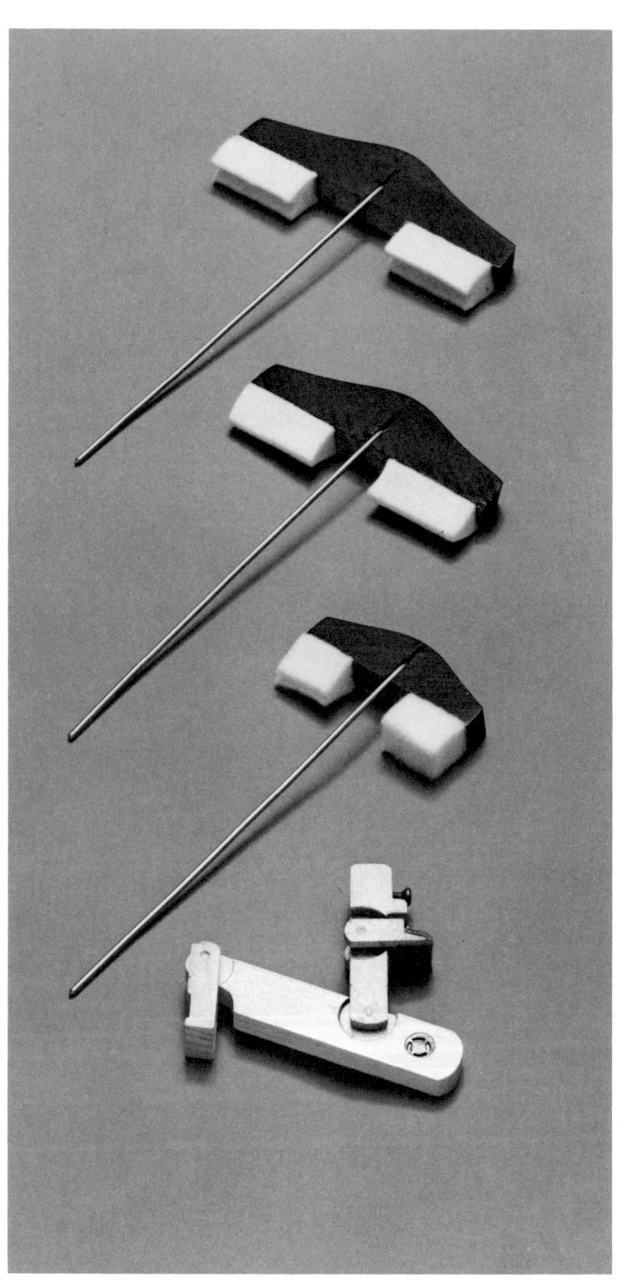

Three dampers and an underlever assembly

Talking About
Pianos

by Corby Kummer

Steinway & Sons
New York

Copyright © 1982 by Steinway & Sons
Steinway Place
Long Island City, N.Y. 11105
Printed in the United States of America
Library of Congress Catalogue Card
Number 81-84064
ISBN 0-9607196-0-1

Contents

Introduction
7

Steinway pianists talk
about their pianos
13

Where pianos and pianists meet
51

Piano teachers talk about
teaching and learning
63

Introduction

"I think we all have the ideal of a piano in our head," says one of the Steinway pianists who talk, in this book, about the mysterious relationship that connects them to the instrument that they play. Anyone who has ever looked for a piano would agree. A great piano is the realization of what every player imagines in his or her inner ear.

What gives the search its mystery is that no two people are alike and no two pianos are alike. In fact, the same piano will sound different when different people play it. Probably no other instrument is so responsive to the mood and personality of the player. And surely no other instrument is described in terms that are so human. Again and again, in these pages, Steinway pianists talk about their pianos in words that are emotional and even intimate.

"It can be tender or dramatic," one says. "The instrument helps me to make contact with myself."

"What I wanted to find," says another, "was a sound that could illuminate a spiritual place within me. Suddenly only one piano was clearly right. I felt that I was all alone in the world with an enormous amount of space to do whatever I wanted."

That, ultimately, is the theme that emerges here:

a piano puts people in touch with their feelings and their deepest longings. Amateurs who play for fun are no less eager than concert artists for this miracle to happen, for "the ideal of a piano" in their head to materialize. The difference is that the concert artists have crystallized what it is that they are looking for—and what they feel when they find it. They have spent a lifetime thinking about it.

The thoughts that the Steinway artists express in this book may surprise the amateur with their originality, their quirkiness, their unexpected dips into confession and metaphor. But none of the thoughts will come as strangers. Everyone who plays the piano seriously has been visited by the same reminders that —in the words of another Steinway pianist—"the piano is an extension of our hands and our hearts."

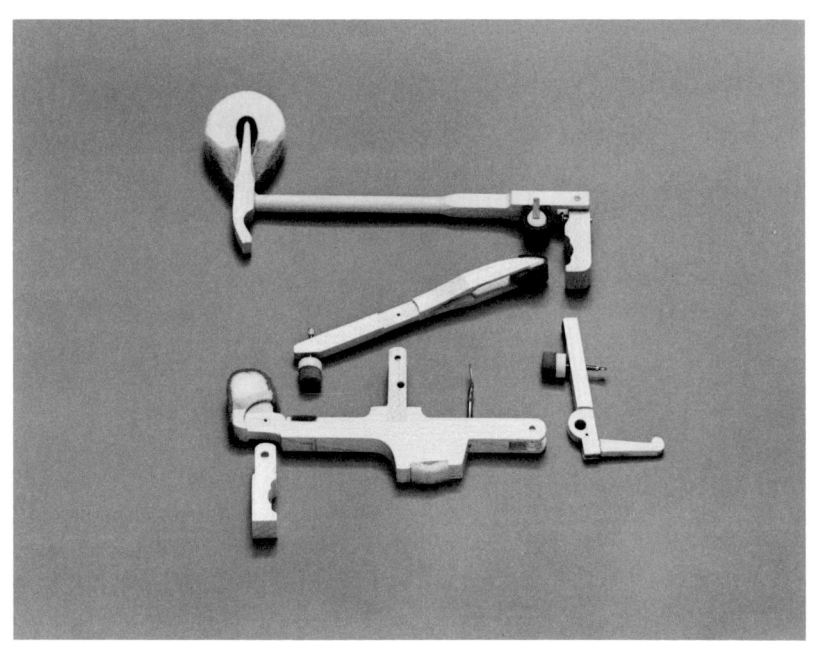

Partial action, disassembled

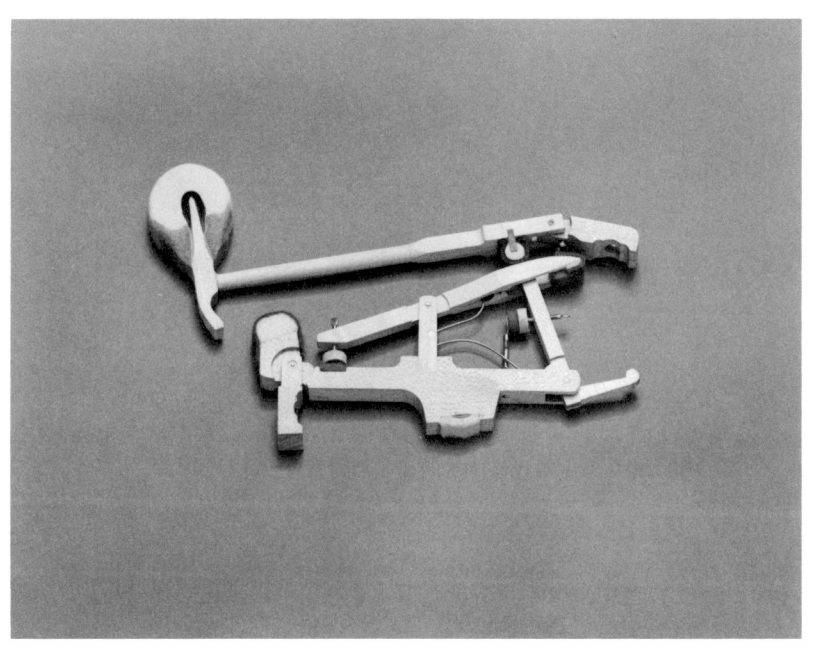

Partial action, assembled

Steinway pianists talk
about their pianos

Rudolf Serkin

I like to play a piano that is beautiful all over, that has a singing quality and brilliance and evenness. If I'm playing a Brahms concerto, I try to find a piano with utmost power that is also tender and light. One should actually play a different piano for each composer on the program. But that's impossible, just as it's unthinkable to play a 100 percent good performance. If you can get 75 percent, I think that's great. I've played many pianos during my career, and for me, the Steinway has it all. Full richness of sound, delicacy, expressiveness—and volume and power.

Things happen in concerts each time that never happen again. I take certain liberties, small liberties, with nuances. I try never to play the same. A good piano can contribute a lot. Sometimes it's hard to know whether one does it oneself or if it just happens.

I'm lucky because I've never felt that the music is not fresh. For me it's always like a first time. The piano I have now is very beautiful, one of the most beautiful I have ever played. We are still discovering each other.

Eugene List

Pianists are always talking about "singing instruments." Naturally I don't think of the piano as a singing instrument because once the sound is produced it begins to die. We cannot sustain a tone or swell on it; we always have to fight against tone decay. But with the use of the pedal, and on a beautifully resonant instrument with a beautiful tone, we can create the illusion that it is a singing instrument. The greatest pianists would make you swear that the piano is singing.

I think we all have an ideal of a piano in our head. It conforms very closely to what our own idea about playing is, and we like to stress in our playing the features that most appeal to us. If you're a poetic player you want a piano with a beautifully modulated tone that has all degrees of brilliance and tenderness. If you're a brilliant player you want a piano that will really deliver the brilliant message. I think actually we're all a combination of the best elements. We all know what we like and which instruments we're most successful with because the instrument, when it's performed on, takes on the coloration of the artist.

I like a piano with a beautiful sound that is not strident in fortissimo, and not so inaudible that the people out front won't hear it. We all like a different degree of resistance. I remember an article in which Benny Goodman's pianist said, "I like a piano that fights back a little bit." I know what he means. You don't want to just blow on the keys and have them go down. You like to have the feeling that you're controlling it.

I also like a piano that has balance. Some pianos are too strong in the bass, which is always a problem because the bass strings are so much longer, and have a lot more power with a lot less effort. You're constantly balancing the treble against the bass.

I think that universities and conservatories don't always protect their good pianos, which sit out where anybody can bang on them. It's incredible what people do to pianos. They use them as ashtrays, spill drinks in them, flick their cigar ashes and throw cigarette butts in them. You always see the sides of pianos burned where people left cigarettes, and rings where they left drinks sitting. It hurts me. I think of the piano as a living thing.

Rosalyn Tureck

The piano is a live creature, certainly. It can be very responsive to one person and not at all to another. There is a deep aesthetic and emotional response to an instrument that you feel is one with you. It's a feeling that one treasures. Even if you get an instrument below that quality it's still your responsibility to produce a performance that is as close to that ideal as possible. I compensate by changing my technique and my touch, from note to note and finger to finger, in lightning seconds. If you have enough technical equipment and tonal sensitivity you can retain a high standard of performance. The greatest fun for me is when I've played a piano that I didn't find ideal, but people tell me afterward that they thought it was a beautiful piano. Some pianos inspire me to do absolutely unpremeditated things in rehearsal or even in performance. The piano is giving back to me, you see. And that's the ideal instrument.

Murray Perahia

There are good pianos that you can give a performance on, but very few pianos that really inspire you. How often does your inner reality correspond to the outer reality? It's chance. I'm grateful when it happens because I experience a special joy that I think only pianists know: communing with music with nothing in between.

Ideally, what you hear in your head should be translated directly to the tips of your fingers. But one has to work on techniques to produce sounds—not just to play fast but to bring out a bass note, for instance, or a contrapuntal melodic line. When I play a phrase on the piano I will try to hear the horn, say, or the oboe, and try to create the same effect on the piano. You have to listen very carefully to orchestras and try to re-create those sounds at home. The more I hear nuances of sound, the more I realize the wealth of colors a pianist must understand and produce. It can be frustrating.

Playing the piano is so much the art of illusion. It's not even so much producing a color as the illusion of a color. The more beautiful your instrument, the more possibilities you have. I think it's important to have a piano in one's own home that one can enjoy playing on, so that one can get pleasure when one is practicing and so inspire one's work. Other pianists, I know, work in the opposite way. But I become attached to certain pianos. After all, I give them my confidences.

Andor Foldes

I'm very happy to have become a pianist because I do everything myself. The singer, the fiddler, the cellist must have an accompanist; a string quartet must have four members; an orchestra can have 100 members who all depend on the conductor. I depend on myself and the piano. If both of them are in order, fine. If not, I'm lost.

The less I know of the action of the piano, the happier I am. I have colleagues who have learned how to tune a piano. Me, I leave the lid on because I don't want to see the innards. I approach the piano in all innocence, start playing, and in a few minutes the piano is mine.

Steven De Groote

I look for a piano that leads itself toward the next note—one that has a certain urgency, a sense of inevitability that the sound must go on. Some pianos have a vertical, static sort of sound, and you have to work, work all the time. Others have a more fluid sound. They pull themselves along. A good piano will do things effortlessly, like a car that does everything right; you don't have to worry about how it's going to take a corner or whether the steering will respond. Other cars just slow you down and you don't get there as fast.

I often listen very closely to how the player of a string instrument is able to swell a note and evolve it.

These are things you can't do on a piano. Some pianos really give you the impression, though, that if you pressed a little harder you actually *would* get more out of a note after you've struck it. In physical terms that's not true, of course, but I'm talking about a quality of sound that swells after the note is played. There are ways to fake a swelling sound if you work hard enough. You're certainly helped along by a piano that's sympathetic.

Horacio Gutiérrez

It sounds funny, but I really feel like a doctor. They say that by just examining the patient briefly, by looking and feeling, a good doctor can tell what's wrong; by just touching and listening I can tell very soon how good a piano is. I have to play only two notes. Seldom have I been fooled. When you play a note it has a kind of blossoming after it's struck. Hearing and judging it is an acquired instinct. It's very personal in most cases, but I think that every great pianist will agree about a really great piano.

I think the kiss of death for any pianist is a dull piano. You can tone down even the most brilliant, awful piano if you have enough control and technique. But a dead piano is hopeless, especially if you're trying to be heard through an orchestra.

I don't think one should become too attached to one's piano, because so much adjustment is necessary during a concert season. Some people have a love affair with their own piano, and I think they're in trouble. They won't be able to have it onstage. I play my own piano rarely; I can experiment on it and see different facets of my own playing.

In some cases during a concert the piano is an antagonist. If you're always worrying about the bass you won't be able to let the music relax you. But a gorgeous piano lets the audience forget about the piano completely—there's no difference between what you're doing and what they're hearing.

Paul Schenly

No instrument can project what you hear in your mind. The minute you think of a performance, and of making people in the last row hear what you're playing at its softest, you're setting limits that don't exist in your mind. I've had wonderful Steinways that have helped me to realize as many of the facets of a piece as I can. But every piano is different, and the music that comes out is like a ray of light that takes on the color of the glass through which it passes. The way I judge my favorite pianos, after picking a beautiful sound and voicing, is by the pedals. To me they are the miracle of the piano, and that's what I love most about a Steinway. You can do things with the pedals that you can't do with any other instrument. That's why a Steinway can adapt itself to more different types of composers and shadings than any other piano I've played.

I remember that the most beautiful sounds I ever heard were at my lessons in Room 226 at the Cleveland Institute of Music. One day I brought in a Schubert sonata from Opus 42 whose notations I had interpreted literally. My teacher said, "You know, at this *portamento* sign in Schubert you use the pedal this way and get a different kind of a sound." Then he played it with the pedal and produced a melting, intoxicating sound that I still dream about. I can never hear that phrase again played any other way.

You never play in the same way twice, of course. You never could. But I believe in having an ideal. Trying to reach it doesn't mean you can't try out a new way of phrasing, or that you can't be spontaneous. It means that every time you play it you're striving for a certain scope, and mood, and climax. If you have perfect acoustics and a responsive audience it helps. But the piano is the most important element. It's an extension of our hands and our heart.

Walter Hautzig

When I was a student I used to sneak into the rehearsals of Arturo Toscanini, and in between vulgarities that would make a truck driver blush he always repeated one word: "*Canta, canta.*" Sing, sing. Well, a piano is my voice: Placido Domingo has his voice, Isaac Stern has his Stradivarius, but I have to change voices and find what will best express my innermost feelings about music. I have found the Steinway the most responsive and satisfying voice.

Hard as it is to find a piano you love, it's useless to complain that you could have done much better on another. It's like a surgeon complaining that he could have operated better with better equipment. Sometimes I think I'm very unhappy with the instrument but end up realizing that it's myself I'm frustrated with. A piano can only sound as good as it's being played.

André Watts

I view the piano as a friend. It's both an extension and a partner. The piano is there to be manipulated by the artist, but it also has its own personality that you can only alter to a certain degree. Some pianos are very aggressive, for instance, and not prone to smile. Some are like very old people whose faces show the lines of a life that has been rough and beautiful: there's a wonderful aliveness beneath a battered surface. Then there is a brand-new piano that is like a person who is extremely competent but who has no soul. I could make a fool of myself with characterizations of pianos. But they are like people.

It's practically impossible to make a pianist genuinely happy with a piano. He always wants an escape hatch, a way to blame the piano for something he's unhappy with. Let's say you get three great pianists and put them in front of an impossibly bad piano. One will say, "This piano is terrible, I can't play on it," and he will get no music out of it. Another will say, "Oh, well, bad piano, just another concert," and it won't sound so terrible, but it won't be very exciting, either. Someone else will say, "Bad piano, but you know right here is a beautiful place and if you trill here it sounds fantastic," and maybe in that person's recital there will be a moment of magic.

I don't like to practice on a wonderful piano because I'll get very happy and then die on the road. But I do like a good piano. You have to stretch your limits and explore what qualities you can get from certain passages. Sometimes when you come to an extraordinary piano you find that an effect you were aiming at, but not achieving, suddenly comes easily. You get other ideas because of the beauty, and every idea will help your conception of the piece, even if the next piano you play isn't as good. For example, before I was 16 the piano I played had 26 strings missing. I wouldn't recommend that to anyone—it's a terrible situation, there's a lot you can't hear. But when I started playing concerts and expected the pianos to be wonderful, I wasn't knocked flat when they weren't.

Pianos change a lot because there are too many of us playing them. We are not always considerate of the colleagues who will follow us into a hall: we find a technician we can browbeat into giving us terribly subjective things that suit our private needs. I don't apologize for my likes and dislikes, but I think it's important for a pianist to admit he has them. There's nothing wrong with saying, "Hey, I don't like this piano." That's your business. But it's not fair to say that a good piano that you don't happen to like is lousy, which too many pianists do. Just say, "It doesn't suit me." That's where all the problems come between pianists and pianos. The big hassle is that there are no absolutes. If there were, it would all be easy.

Ivan Moravec

I think that if you put ten pianists in the same room with the same choice of pianos, all or nearly all of them would choose the same piano. We all look for a perfectly regulated action and an even sound. What we most want in a piano is not such a mystery, you know.

Unfortunately, even if you find a beautiful piano the sound changes from morning to night. I made two recordings many years ago in Vienna on a beautiful instrument. I came back a year later and found that I couldn't use it because it had completely lost its voice. How do you explain it? Perhaps somebody complained that it was too bright, or too strong, and they voiced it differently.

The really individual choice a pianist makes is of the action. Even if the pianos he has to choose from are identically regulated, one pianist will want an easy action, the other a hard action. A responsive action that suits the artist is of the utmost importance, and I've never found a better action than the Steinway's.

Roger Williams

Other companies have tried to copy the action of the Steinway, and they've done a pretty good job. They use the same kind of wood and everything else, but they can't duplicate the soul that the Steinway has. It brings out whatever you have that is extra and special. You'll all of a sudden find yourself playing things that you never would play on another piano. And of course the tone of the Steinway is superior to any piano that's ever been made.

I think that I have in my house the world's finest piano. It was Rubinstein's favorite, and it took me many years and a lot of conniving to purchase. I can't imagine a more responsive piano. I can express any mood that I know on it. That's what's so wonderful about a piano. It can take a beating or it can take a loving, and it doesn't talk back. Beats any woman in the world.

Eugene Istomin

I most often choose power, because the more powerful the instrument, the more possibilities you have in controlling the range of dynamics without forcing it. It's easy to overplay a powerful piano. You have to avoid banging. A safer choice is a piano with a smaller dynamic range, but then you wind up with a kind of polite instrument.

I'm always concerned with the octave that starts an octave above middle C because that's where almost all the tunes are played. It's easy to find a good middle or high register and a rich, carrying bass, which the Steinway is famous for. But if I find a piano where that particular octave sings, I'll take it in a minute.

We are different artists on pianos that we're not comfortable on. The public doesn't know that, because professional artists have ways of hiding it. But when an instrument inspires you to give, you become involved. The process isn't erotic, exactly, but it's certainly terribly physical. Obtaining satisfaction from an instrument that gives to you willingly is different from obtaining it by rape or by using tremendous discipline. I remember Rubinstein once saying that he liked an instrument that challenged him: *he* would get it to do what he wanted, like another conquest with the ladies.

I don't really believe in that. The instrument is not a lady one is seducing: some abstract listener might be the lady, perhaps. But the instrument is an extension of one's self, and the body rejects certain instruments the way it rejects certain transplanted organs. The ideal is when the piano is a natural part of the pianist. I have found pianos that to touch and to play were sheer ecstasy.

Emanuel Ax

The first time I played a concert grand was at Carnegie Hall when I was 13. The hall was empty, and a friend let me in. I hadn't thought I could play well at all, but all of a sudden I found out that I had a lot more technique than I thought I did. Just being able to play runs evenly, for instance. I still look for a piano that's even, which means that it's properly voiced. Voicing is a matter of how hard or soft the hammers are when they hit the strings. If they're all very hard the piano produces a brilliant sound. If they're all very soft it produces a more muffled sound. If they're not even, you have to memorize which note is dead and which note is live. Muffled pianos are a big problem. You have to force them. The more variety in a piano, the better I like it. I'll always pick the piano that can produce the greatest number of different sounds.

Ilana Vered

I like pianos that have a talkative sound. I know exactly what I want in my head and only sometimes find it. The sound must penetrate. The piano has to have a brilliant top and the most gorgeous bass. I love colorings, and it must help me to reproduce them without being so hard to play that I have to work ten hours a day on my technique. And then it has to have an aura of magic about it. That's all.

I haven't found an ideal piano. But even though you never find in one person everything you want, you make that person beloved. So I find a piano that has one or two of the ingredients I want and make it into my ideal. If I can talk with that tone, everything else is possible. When I'm playing I don't want to hear a piano. I can't stand to hear a piano sound. It must be something beyond a piano. I hear in my head a violin or a voice, a cello or a flute. Not a piano.

I don't get bogged down in technical details because I don't think a performance should be 100 percent perfect. I'm just human, and if people are going to feel something at my performance it won't be whether one C sharp is exactly regulated. I almost don't think about technique anymore, I'm so concerned about tone. Maybe it's because I played on so many bad pianos throughout my life, especially horrendous ones in Israel, and I wasn't spoiled.

I don't think it's a good idea to sit at home and play one piano forever, learning how to manipulate it and make it respond to you. When you go out on a tour it's a jungle. I like to go down to the Steinway basement just to play other pianos so I won't get the response I'm used to. An artist has to play as often as he can on as many pianos as he can. No two pianos are ever alike.

Alicia de Larrocha

When I was young I was attached to my own piano and enjoyed everything about it. Youth, youth—everything is beautiful when you are young, and little by little you see that some of the things you thought were beautiful aren't really. Now I find it difficult to find a very good piano because I have such small hands. When I find an action that is comfortable, the tone is usually too thin because the hammers are smaller, and so the sound is smaller, too. I need a big tone and a very long sound that keeps singing for a long time.

For practice it's another thing. Practice means hard work, and at home I like a stiff piano with a deep action because I have to push it very hard. I seldom play my own piano for pleasure, unfortunately. In addition to everything, I am a housewife and mother, and often I play two notes and go to the kitchen, or two more notes and the telephone rings.

Very often I say, "Oh, another concert! I cannot do it, I will be unable to play, I am so tired." But then I start, and I listen to myself. I always say that I can do better with a normal piano and beautiful acoustics than with a beautiful piano and bad acoustics. Many pianists, for instance, say, "This piano is terrible. It's so stiff! So hard to play!" I say, "It's hard to play? Just play pianissimo. Is it stiff now?" They say, "Oh, no." It's a matter of being able to hear yourself, and if you have to push very hard just to get sound, it's terrible. So if I have both beautiful acoustics and a beautiful piano I'm very happy. Even if I thought I was exhausted I find that I like what I'm hearing, and the expression comes.

Rudolf Firkusny

I like playing different pianos often because the differences give you new ideas and can even change your interpretation. If a piano is responding ideally it is an inspiration—it makes you feel that you are doing something you always wanted to do but hadn't succeeded at. Any piano that lets you express what you want to is joyous. We perform with all our heart and all our soul and naturally we are helped by our instrument. I have always played Steinway and still love it very much. It fulfills most of my wishes and desires.

Charles Wadsworth

I lost interest early in being a solo pianist. There's no pleasure in walking out to play a lone nine-foot-long piano all by myself—it's close to torture. But if you walk out and you've got Pinky Zukerman there and you're going to play a Brahms sonata for violin and piano, you're happy. Playing with other people is different from playing alone because you're very far ahead in your thinking. You're always anticipating what the other players will be doing, adjusting and giving them inspiration. So you want to be able to rely on the piano to give you the quality of sound that you want. The best concerts I'v ever played have been on pianos that had that reliability.

   I want to hear the piano say, "I'm unique as an instrument." I like to find an individual personality in the piano that makes it especially beautiful. That often means probing the upper and middle registers, which is where your beautiful, melodic stuff goes on. I've always been inclined to go for a sweet, dulcet quality in the upper register instead of something brilliant. Often I choose a piano based on the piece I'll play. If there's a scherzo movement with a lot of very fast repetition, for example, I'll take something with a fast action and trust to luck that it will be beautifully tuned and that I can do as much with the tone as possible. Ideally, you don't want to be aware that you are playing an instrument. With a great piano you have an immediate extension of whatever you want from your mind through your fingers: you touch the instrument and it does it for you.

   Sometimes you get upset on the day of performance

because you're sure that the instrument has changed from the day before. That's a case of nerves, I've come to realize. I'll play the first piece of the concert and be horrified, thinking, "This is the worst-tuned instrument I've ever played." During the second piece I'm more relaxed, and by the end of the concert the piano sounds perfectly fine.

Ken Noda

I believe that the piano is the most difficult instrument of all because your fingers are the members of the orchestra, and you have to control them and make what they do sound balanced. I would rather keep a piece in my head musically, not pianistically. If you don't have the proper agility or depth of color, you obviously won't be able to express what you feel: so when you're practicing, it's important to realize what you're doing with your hands and to become involved in the technical part of playing. But once the performance comes you have to forget about all that and just think of the music itself. Otherwise it's like practicing in front of an audience.

Misha Dichter

I used to be content with mellow, round tones, but my taste in pianos has changed. Now I need extroverted pianos that offer the greatest possible dynamic range without being strident. At home I need a workhorse piano. My own has muted voices so that when I get to concert halls I can be happily surprised—which I am three out of a hundred times. If I were a total perfectionist I would say "Forget it" at least 85 percent of the time. Yet I have to reconcile myself to the fact that the audience can't tell beyond the fourth row if one note goes down harder than another. I have only a superficial idea of how a piano actually works. But I knew enough to pack filing and voicing tools on one tour so that I could file down the hammers for Beethoven's Fourth. I had to do it by candlelight at midnight because the next pianist would be furious.

If I go to a hall with a special piano, though, I'm in a great mood. I know what it and I are capable of, so I almost feel that I'm sitting back and listening to the concert. A perfectly regulated piano enables me to forget the technical side of piano playing: the piano will do anything, go with me anywhere, and I have flights of fancy that make me say later, "I never thought that passage could take wing." And the piano was responsible.

Pianists are famous for getting together and talking about their favorite pianos as if they were old girl friends. "Twenty-three," we'll sigh. "What an upper register!"

Vladimir Ashkenazy

I don't think there is an ideal piano that would suit every piece you play. You might as well ask me what composers I like best; I can't tell you—I like so many, and for different types of music you need different types of pianos. I love a very beautiful, round sound in the middle register, for instance, but sometimes that isn't suitable for music that requires a different kind of sound. The piano only helps or doesn't help, really. It's the music that's most important. I think people often forget that we are musicians first and instrumentalists second.

James Tocco

When I decided to buy a piano I first looked for a used one, thinking that I couldn't afford a new one. I tried a lot of the Steinways and some of them were quite nice. For comparison I decided to go to the Steinway showroom and try a few new ones. There were five or six there, and the second piano I tried turned out to be such a beautiful instrument that I literally couldn't stop playing it. I spent a couple of hours there playing everything imaginable, and I became fascinated with the evenness in the scale from bottom to top. The voicing was very responsive. I fell in love with the possibilities of combinations I could get out of it. I said to my wife, "We've got to have this instrument," and it's still as beautiful today. I don't think I'll ever finish exploring its possibilities.

Grant Johannesen

The people at Steinway have always been very careful to claim that there is a Steinway sound but *not* a Steinway tone. The distinction is very important. The artist is the one who is going to make the piano sing for him. Tone is created in the head and somehow washes down and comes out of your hands. So when we talk about wanting the piano with the best tone, it's really a cop-out. Tone, by the way, never comes out on a recording. The engineer manipulates the sound too much and you never hear that marvelous peculiarity of tone. Maybe with digital recording we'll get a more personal sound.

What I've always loved about the Steinway is that it gets better as it gets older. Most other pianos are at their best when they're new. I've played on any number of Steinways that were perfectly calibrated to my needs, but you can't expect those every day of the year. Wood lives, you know—it breathes like human beings and consequently the piano has its off days and on days. It's very fashionable today to complain about pianos, but we're not going to let the public down just because we don't like the instrument. I don't see how we can blame a bad concert on a piano.

Most pianists of the last hundred years have played the Steinway, and if they didn't start with it they ended up with it. There must be a reason why serious artists have chosen to play this instrument, which is harder to play than others. Probably they all realized that it offers so much more. No other piano can accommodate all composers so well.

Alan Marks

Recently I was choosing a piano for a concert. I played four of the pianos I could choose from for about 20 seconds each, and liked one right away. But then I played different passages from different pieces to test the real responses that each piano had, and was totally confused. Each instrument had its own character, and each worked—in a different way. For about 15 minutes all four sounded wonderful.

Then I played the music most personal to me, the second movement of one of the Schubert sonatas, to find how much of my own imagination I could let loose. What I wanted to find was a sound that could illuminate a spiritual place within me. Suddenly only one piano was clearly right. I felt that I was all alone in the world with an enormous amount of space to do whatever I wanted. It's like striking up a relationship with a person—sometimes there's a chemistry that you can't fathom or articulate.

I love my own piano—I must have gone back to the showroom 20 times before I found one that I knew by instinct was right. But I also like working on uprights because I enjoy the challenge of an instrument that won't do very much. Sometimes I do even better practicing on a really bad piano. But I always look forward to coming home to my own.

On some days I just look at this big black thing sitting there and I feel that it's Pandora's box. It can be hard to sit and face it. I feel that it has a real presence, a real force. I know it can be tender, dramatic or troubled. Of course these are all my own feelings; but the piano, not my body, is my instrument, and I have to make it an extension of myself. Sometimes I feel that the instrument helps me to make contact with myself. Other times I can't come through. Under the best circumstances I feel that I'm hand in hand with it. A performance is realized through a piano, after all, and there has to be some kind of meeting, rather than me imposing myself on the instrument and trying to force it to do things it simply can't do.

At other times it can be a real friend, a consolation. I don't like to use the piano that way in a performance, but if I'm troubled the piano is where I want to go. The most joyous playing for me is the deepest, not the happiest. Exuberance and exhilaration may come after the fact, but the joy comes when I can be the most honest with myself, and that's hard. Only once or twice have I had the experience of feeling something so deep and so untouched that I could go on and on and on with no sense of fatigue, no sense of being spent or of spending. I feel most alive in those moments. Often in a concert there's a moment like that: it doesn't last too long, maybe a movement at most. When it comes there's an absolute quiet and a transcendence of time. In those moments the quality of the piano has a great deal to do with my being able to reach those high places.

Vladimir Horowitz

You can't play the piano in black and white, just as it is. The ideal artist knows how to produce the most colors. The piano is a tool. It's a dead instrument, a piece of wood. We have to extract something from it. The piano is my mouth, my ear, my heart, my head. If it gives me freedom I can talk through it to my audience. I look for continuity of tone, which is a matter of adjusting the dampers, and for proper adjustment of the pedal, which is the heart of the piano, like our heart beating. Before I traveled with my own piano I would play in small towns and a string would go out. That can happen any time. But once in the '40s the pedal went off in the middle of the concert. There was no technician, so they closed the curtain and my wife fixed it herself. Now I don't go to very small towns. I have my own piano—I am very attached to it, I know it. When I left Russia for Berlin in 1925, I went to all the makers and tried all the pianos. I struck on Steinway and I never changed. Never.

Now my dream is to have the ideal hall—and audience. There are three kinds of audience. One is social; they come because the artist is well known and they have to be seen. That's the worst. They're asleep from beginning to end and don't know what's going on. Then there are the professionals who listen only to the notes to see if there is a mistake. They don't listen to the music. My father-in-law, Maestro Toscanini, used to say that for a mistake you never go to jail. The third is the best audience. They come because they want to hear me, they believe in me, and they want to hear the best. Sometimes I don't give the best, but they will come again because they know it wasn't my night.

I can tell what kind of audience I have by how they listen. Applause doesn't mean anything. Silence is the success of the artist. If they listen to every note and don't cough too much or move or rustle their programs, they are attentive. The concentration of the artist is contagious to the public, and the public starts to be a little hypnotized. They're listening to the music, not just to the notes and whether you play too fast or too slow. That's secondary. That's for the critics to show that they know something. The artistry you cannot erase.

I discover things on the stage. I don't know what will happen in the concert. I never play the same twice. Never. Because I listen to what I play and how the piano sounds in the different halls. I can improvise interpretation on the stage. You have the architecture —you have a house. The house stays there, but you can make the rooms different. I am talking about details; the architecture of the piece is always the same. At some concerts I am really more satisfied with certain pieces. I get tired sometimes, sometimes I don't sleep so well, everything counts. I try to do my best, and if my best is not the best for me I am very much disturbed. Well, sometimes the public doesn't know it; neither do the critics.

I never miss a day of practicing. Sometimes I need calisthenics and nothing else. Two hours is really too much practicing. Like any exercise, if you do it every day you don't need to do it for that long. Enough for one day. Next day will be better. Don't rush; it will always come, but keep going. The result is the same if it takes two weeks instead of three days. If you work seven hours a day for a week, your soul goes mechanical, too. I don't practice on the piano that I use for concerts. It would just make it old. I want to keep it fresh.

Young artists today listen to records and want to play like the artist. They don't try to play like themselves. I never listen to my own records. I don't play the way I did ten years ago, so why should I? Sometimes on the radio I'll recognize my playing. Sometimes I'm wrong. The only pianists I listen to are of the old generation, Rachmaninoff especially. He didn't sound like anyone else. Only like himself. I don't take students who come in and want to imitate me. The teacher should be a conductor. A conductor doesn't take a flute or a clarinet and show someone how to play it. He tells them what they have to do and they have to find out how. If the pianist is not intelligent enough to understand what the teacher says, he'll never be able to do it. But everybody wants the easy way; it's much easier than the hard way.

I love everything which is difficult. I love something unusual, something that is like the voice. You have a beautiful piano in perfect condition and strike a nice two notes. But that isn't enough, not for a concert. You have to vary things from composer to composer, from century to century. I try to make the piano sound like it's not a piano. It can be a violin, a piccolo, a string ensemble, a woodwind quartet—anything but a piano.

Gary Graffman

I want a piano to have a long-lasting sound. Some pianos are more percussive than others, and the sound drops immediately to a quarter of what it was when the key was struck. I like a piano that makes the sound seem to disappear gradually. Few pianos have that naturally. I also want a gorgeous bass with an equally good upper register, and it can be hard to find both. Usually the problem is that you find a potentially good piano but it needs voicing—the hammers have to be picked or filed—and regulating. So you have to plan the whole performance around the first E above middle C and the second G sharp above middle C because they're less brilliant than their neighboring notes. And if that's all you think about during the performance you're not going to think about the performance very much. If Heifetz plays on some terrible violin he'll make it sound better than the kid who was practicing on it, but he won't sound like Heifetz. In New York you have a huge choice of pianos and reserve them sometimes two years ahead.

I'm very attached to one of my Steinways. It's exactly the same age I am. The Curtis Institute of Music lent it to me when I was seven. When I was 17 they sold it to my father for $500—quite a low price, even in 1946—because they weren't allowed to give away loan instruments. I immediately had it completely rebuilt at the Steinway factory, and it was beautiful. I had it rebuilt again a few years ago. It's been with me 44 years. I wouldn't ever give it up.

Lili Kraus

I'm a daredevil by nature, and I will take the risk of choosing a piano that is tough going in order to get the beauty of sound I want. Ideally, of course, I would choose the instrument that best speaks my language, which is one of infinite articulation and tremendous precision with a shiny treble and a powerful bass. In 1965 I bought a Steinway to prepare a Mozart concerto that I had to record. It wasn't seasoned in any way. It wasn't painted, even: it looked like a piece of raw wood, a monster. Ugh, how I hated it. It was stiff, it was lifeless, it was terrible. I had to conquer it. By and by it yielded, and now I wouldn't part with that piano for anything in the world. I miss it when I'm away, but I miss a piano as I miss my family: I adore them, I long for them, but they cannot actually be present in my day-to-day life.

Every time I play it the Steinway teaches me something. You have a hypnotic vision of a chord—for instance, the first chord of the Beethoven G major Concerto, which is one of the most difficult beginnings imaginable. Without the piano's help you couldn't approach, let alone materialize, that sound you imagine. So you materialize it; but that is not good enough, so you go further, and the Steinway goes with you—and goes ahead of you, and falls short when you fall short. It's a very complex and miraculous procedure.

Claudio Arrau

I want a piano at home that is rather heavy and makes me work hard, because then it is wonderful to perform in concert on a piano with a light action. One should be able to play well on even the worst piano, they always say, and I do think one can do something with a bad piano. One has all sorts of resources to use in that case.

I don't know what it is, but pianos seem to have improved in recent years, in both America and Europe. I still think that Steinways are the best pianos ever made in the world.

Charles Rosen

I like a piano that gives you the impression of a very beautiful balance of tones instead of just a great many bright, high overtones that predominate. I also prefer a long diminuendo in the middle register that gives you the impression of great sustaining power, so that you can play the piano very softly and every one of the notes will last. I dislike soft pianos. Usually the pianos I like turn out to be hard to play, unfortunately. In many cases the technician is actually more important than the piano. With the help of a marvelous technician you can bring out the best in any piano. There are always compromises. But I've played on pianos that were fairly close to ideal.

I believe the old line that there are no bad pianos, only bad pianists. A really good pianist can do something even with an instrument that isn't all he would like. I always like to spend time practicing on the piano I'll play at a concert, to see whether I'm going to have to make a special effort or whether it's going to go all by itself.

In a great many pieces the pianist must think in terms of other instruments. A lot of Mozart, for instance, is written the way a singer would sing: it imitates the vocal effects in opera. So if you play the passages in Mozart that imitate the vocal leads of a soprano, for instance, you have to make them sound as if it were a little hard to get from one note to another. The whole effect is of that slight effort that the soprano makes to get from a very low note to a high note. Many Scarlatti pieces are supposed to sound like the guitar, but they were written for the harpsichord. So if you play them on the piano it's twice removed and that much harder. Often in playing Liszt or Paganini you must make the piano sound like a violin.

But I could never take up another instrument. I enjoy the piano too much.

Melvin Stecher and Norman Horowitz

NH: I think both of us look first for beauty of tone and subtlety of sound.

MS: After the sound, the action is very important to me. That's where the two of us differ. Norman has a much larger hand than I do, yet I prefer the harder action. When I play I love to feel that I'm fighting something.

NH: When we pick pianos we try to find two that will blend well. We wouldn't take one that had a different kind of tone from the other.

MS: No two pianos will ever be exactly alike, of course. But if one piano is brighter than the other, that's fine because we'll put the piano in the position where we need a bright piano. We've learned over the years to take the lid off the bright piano, which we put behind "piano number one," where a solo piano usually is. It's amazing how many people think we're playing one instrument with two keyboards. At least a dozen people always come onstage afterward and creep around the pianos to see how they're put together.

NH: When the piano is as responsive as the Steinway has been for us, some of the things we do are hair-raising. Sometimes we will make nuances and take dynamic changes without even discussing them: all of a sudden we feel that what is happening is probably the most spectacular thing we've done in a long time. That's the excitement of any concert. Sometimes we'll suddenly pull back with a tremendous rubato or a dynamic contrast, and we ourselves will be shocked that we were able to do it with such control.

MS: Or pleased.

NH: You can only do that when you're playing on an instrument that you can mold as carefully as clay.

Arthur Rubinstein

The ideal piano absolutely answers your way of playing and your fingerwork. Some pianos respond to me right away and make people say, "Ach, ach, how you play, it sounds so divine, as if you were singing." I must tell you, a piano that is the ideal for one man is quite the contrary for another. I know very well the pianos Horowitz uses. While I was in New York recently he very very charmingly sent me a piano of his for a week or two. A pupil of mine who came could hardly play anything, it was so hard to play.

Pianos have a personality, you know. I can recognize one piano among a dozen—I did, in fact, because in Paris I had to send my own concert grand to Germany to be repaired. When I flew to Hamburg there were about 15 pianos lined up, and they said, "We repaired your piano, and we are very curious to know if you recognize yours." Well, I went through six or seven, and stopped at mine. "You guessed it," they said.

Some pianos don't let me give my best. The public is very, very sensitive, and they feel it immediately if the artist is not at ease. If the artist comes out and goes to the piano with fear, the audience is dominating him. They're saying, "Let's see what he can do." The artist must come out instead saying, "I can do my best on this piano—you listen to me," and ah! Then you get it, you get everything you want.

Mona Golabek

When you spend five to ten hours a day connected to something else, you almost don't feel at home when you're away from it. It's like an extension of yourself, the other half of your soul. I've been told that I treat the instrument as if it were alive. I guess I do see it as my pal. Maybe a healthy person would say, "I'm complete without it: I am a human being first, then I am a pianist." But in truth I think we define ourselves first as instrumentalists. We all take pride in what we've spent our lives cultivating. And if something were to happen to me that would make me unable to play, it would be like the death of half of myself. It would take enormous spirit to channel all those artistic or creative energies into something new. I would always feel empty somewhere.

Nosebolt nut   *Keylid pivot plate*

                                   Three agraffes

Lyre pedal rod nut

Action frame dome

                                   Treble keyblock plate

                                   Bass keyblock plate

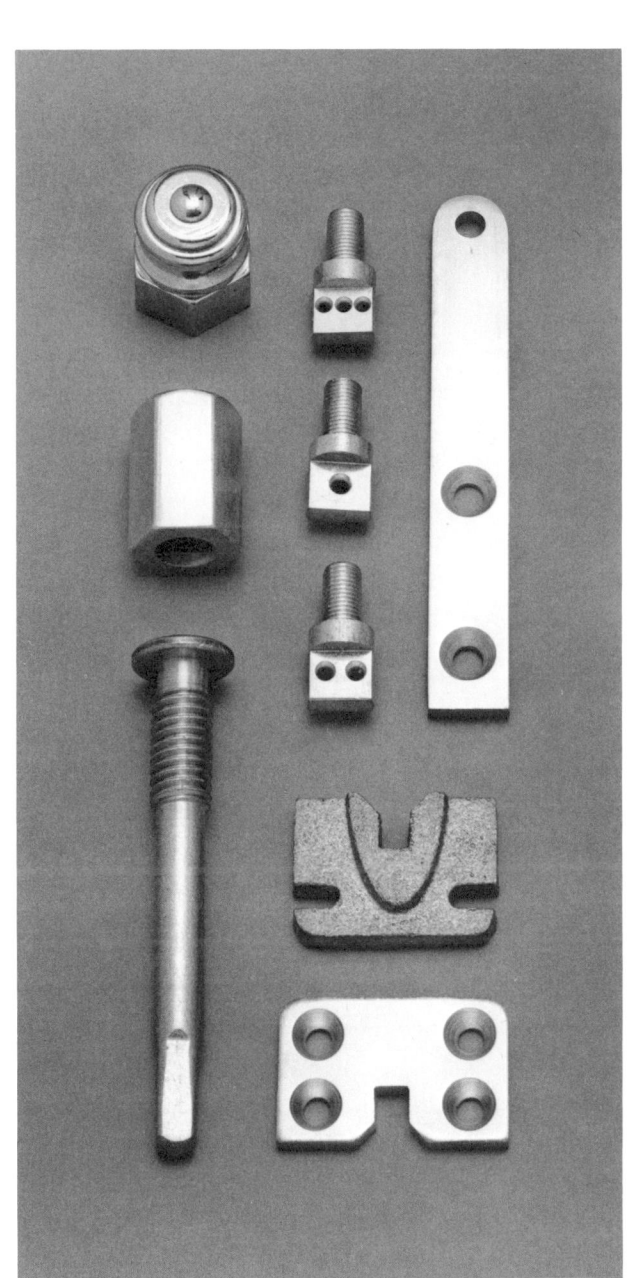

Where pianos and pianists meet

Where pianos and pianists meet

Great pianos and great pianists meet in a large room in Steinway Hall, on West 57th Street, in New York. Called simply "the basement," it looks in fact something like a basketball court. The floors are parquet, the walls are cinderblock, and rows of pipes line the ceiling. Fluorescent lamps illuminate workbenches littered with tools and disembodied piano actions. It is here that artists, selecting the pianos that they will use in concerts, make some of the most beautiful music in the world.

The lucky eavesdropper most likely to be working in a corner is one of the four concert technicians employed by Steinway to prepare the pianos that the artists choose. Days start early for the "tuners," as the concert technicians call themselves. They usually arrive by 7 o'clock, and on a typical morning all but one are tuning pianos in different recital halls by 9:15. "There is only one way to regulate a piano," the remaining tuner, dressed in a white coat, says. "Though they all come from our two factories, each piano feels and sounds different—for reasons that are hard to explain. Some are simply beautiful but have a smaller sound than others. You must feel how far you can go in making tone. It's always a challenge to find what we can get out of a piano. Some take a few weeks or even months before they are ready for concerts. I'll put a new piano in a corner, and artists will break it in by banging on it for hours."

This baptism by violence is an old tradition. A new piano can rarely be used for a concert before it has been played—hard—for many hours. Some of the pianos designated for concert use will stay in the basement, being coddled and seasoned until the tuners agree that they are ready to be used onstage. Others will go to the 135 other Steinway dealers across America who maintain pianos for visiting artists to use in a performance. Altogether, Steinway reserves for concerts 305 pianos, worth more than $7 million. Artists or their agents must pay for moving and tuning, but not for the use of the piano.

Pianos change after they have been played for a while, and the tuner who chooses a piano at the factory hopes that it will gradually fulfill its promise, becoming richer and more complex. Sometimes he is disappointed, and the piano goes back to the factory for more work. But if a piano fails to meet the expectations of an artist, it won't be from the tuner's lack of effort. "The best piano is not good if it is not properly tuned and regulated," the tuner says, going to the piano that is his morning's work.

He slips out the action, lifting it onto his wooden workbench. "I always check the action first, even in a concert hall," he says, "because it's all wood and felt and buckskin, and humidity or being moved too much can change the tone." The action includes the keyboard and the hammers that are attached to each key. An intricate mechanism under each hammer accelerates the motion of the hammer, catches it as it rebounds from the strings, and holds it in position for the next striking. Before the tuner puts the action back in the piano he tests each of the 88 mechanisms, making sure that they function properly and match their neighbors. He makes small adjustments to the thin wires and the nearly hidden screws, using an arsenal of tools whose smallness, precision and oddity make them more suited to a medieval alchemist or, perhaps, an exceptionally sadistic dentist. (The tools are so specialized, in fact, that a tuner often designs his own). Finally he makes sure that the keys are level and that they require exactly the same pressure to push down; he checks each one with a small gold weight.

Once the action is regulated, the tuner reinstalls it and starts to tune the piano. First he must be sure that the strings that the hammer strikes for each note are in unison and at the proper pitch. There are three strings per note in the treble, two per note in the tenor and one per note in the bass. Any decent tuner can manage this step, the Steinway tuner explains; the secret is to keep the strings in place after the tuner has put his hammer on the tuning pin of the next note. "The tuning pin and string must be placed absolutely solidly so the note won't go out of tune," he says, striking a note. "It's easy to set the pin. But it has to stay there once the tuning hammer is removed. If the tuner doesn't know how to set the pin properly, the piano will never sound just right." He takes off the tuning hammer and strikes the note, which is still in tune.

The last step, tone regulating or "voicing," requires

the most subtlety, and the concert technicians at Steinway try to save it for a time when they can consult the artist before they begin. In many cases the technician is so familiar with the artist's tastes that he knows exactly what he or she needs, and it is this instinct that guides the technician's selection of pianos for the artist to try. Few artists trust the house pianos that are available in every hall. "They automatically think they're bad," the tuner says, "even when they're not. One exception is Alfred Brendel. I voiced a house piano for him recently as well as I could, and he got fantastic sound out of it. A great artist is able to get a beautiful sound out of a . . . " He gestures, searching for the worst epithet he can use. "Out of a worn-out action!"

Four pianos are due back before noon, two to be offered to an artist who will visit late in the day. Deciding which piano is right for which artist is a matter of sound and feel, the tuner says. "If the artist has to labor hard to produce the sound he wants, he shouldn't use that piano, even though it might be a good instrument."

A visit from an artist is a happy occasion—one that the technicians and the staff look forward to. All of them brighten, for example, when Alicia de Larrocha arrives on a Wednesday to select pianos for concerts that she will give at the Metropolitan Museum of Art and at Avery Fisher Hall in New York. Of the ten pianos lined neatly in the basement, three have been left open for Miss de Larrocha. "It's confusing to an artist if you show him too many," the tuner says.

Miss de Larrocha, an animated and elegantly dressed woman, sits first at number CD 409, a piano she has played before and a favorite of many artists. Each piano is numbered and coded—CD for a nine-foot piano, CB for a seven-foot—in the sort of gold decal type that frequently appears on office doors. The number is affixed on top of the hinged cover flap that is folded back when the piano is played. She pauses at the concert stool, straightens her back, then sits and begins to play rippling passages from a Mozart sonata that she will play at the museum. Satisfied, she stops short and begins a dramatic passage from a Schubert sonata to test the strength of her forte. As she increases the intensity of the passage her lavender knit jacket slips slowly from her shoulders, which are trembling. The passage grows even louder, and one wonders how so much power can come from so small a body until, as she leans into the keyboard, one sees how wide her shoulders are.

She stops abruptly and rises to throw her jacket onto a nearby chair. In contrast to the thundering passage, she begins playing pianissimo and looks at the tuner with fond rebuke. He had told her that CD 409 was in the same condition as it was the last time she played it. "They have done something to it," she says. "Needles? Voicing? The hammers?" Without waiting for an answer she rises and asks to see a closed piano at the end of the room.

"That's against the wall," the tuner warns, "and you know that distorts the tone."

"I will just try the action," Miss de Larrocha says, waving away the tuner, who moves to raise the top of the piano. "I can tell." The tuner unlocks the keyboard and she begins to play the same passages.

The sound of this piano, even discounting its proximity to the wall, pleases her. Miss de Larrocha plays several of the more lush passages from the Schubert and rises. "Yes," she says, beaming. "It is bigger. Better for Fisher." Her manager suggests that to become comfortable with it she should also use this piano for her concert at the Metropolitan Museum. "The sound is too big," she explains. "And the pianissimo is so beautiful on 409." Unable to resist testing the new piano, however, she darts back to it and plays a trilling passage from Mozart in the upper register. She smiles. "I'll use it at the Metropolitan, too," she says.

The tuner marks her choice in his log, and the pleasure on his face as he escorts Miss de Larrocha through the enormous steel door is almost guilty. This has been one of the many mornings, after all, when he has listened—as part of his job—to the kind of piano playing that most people only dream of hearing.

Duplex scale

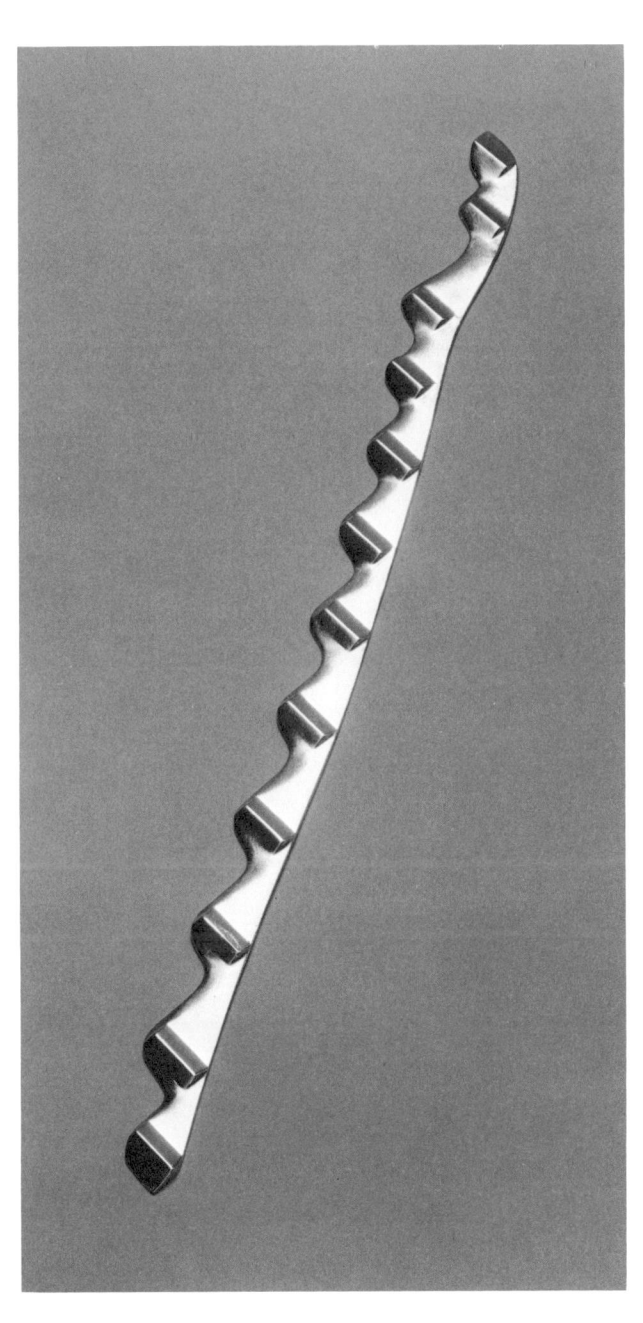

Piano teachers talk about
teaching and learning

Piano teachers talk about teaching and learning

"A student may be good at coordination, speed and endurance, and yet not be a poet," says William Masselos, who teaches piano at the Juilliard School of Music. "A fine musician will make you laugh and weep and all sorts of things. I look for something in a student that speaks from inside. If he has music in his soul he might as well let it out."

Most of the students who audition for Jeannette Haien privately or at the Mannes College of Music dismay her. "These poor kids are dragged on tour and bring forth their *shticks*," she says. "They play their études, and the parents and teachers smile, thinking it's so wonderful. But you *know* instantly when the mind is struggling—when it won't yield to a facile interpretation." Miss Haien suspects that most "prodigies" lack musicality. "There is a clear separation between musical athletes and artists," she says. "With athletes you know you're going to a marathon. Artists force you to think as the performance happens. They evoke a visceral response."

These teachers take for granted a student's "equipment," the fruit of the years he spent learning to make the fingers play the printed notes. However, Jeaneane Dowis, who teaches privately, is most interested in solving problems of technical difficulty, and experienced pianists often come to her for advice. "When I was a student I used to *beg* people to teach me technique," she says. "But nobody would. The teachers I had certainly never started by saying, as I do, that the first thing to think about is *ease*." She goes to her piano and puts her hands on the keyboard with an exaggerated arch. "Wrists held high are an anathema," she says. "We have an atavistic fear of lifting our fingers. I think John Thompson should be buried in hot coals." Thompson, in his popular series of piano instruction books, advocates a highly arched hand with the fingers lined up in a row. "The palm should be level with the keyboard, the knuckles and fingers flat." When Miss Dowis's son was born, she says, she was the only new mother at the hospital who looked first at her child's hands. "The first time he sat at the piano Edward had a perfect picture-postcard hand position," she says proudly. "Nice and flat."

When new students come to Miss Dowis, she feels their arm and hand muscles while they play if she hears a "choked" sound. "I often feel funny pulls on people's fingers," she says. "From there I work on their shoulders, body and legs." The most painful problems, she says, result from the pianist's ignorance about his own body. "If someone has an image that his arm ends at his shoulder, for instance, he'll be very stiff. So many people injure themselves by not learning to play properly." She recalls a young Israeli pianist who required only a minor adjustment of the way she held her hand to relieve the chronic pain she had suffered; yet she refused to change. "The whole idea that she had spent her life holding her hand in the wrong position was too much for her.

"My unfavorite position," Miss Dowis says, "is low elbows, which make an ugly sound that hits and dies." Imitating a student who recently played for her, she screws her face into a grimace. "My teacher, Rosina Lhevinne, used to say that if you attack the piano it will attack you. You have to learn to work *with* the piano, not against it." She caresses the keyboard delicately. "One school feels that you must stroke the piano as if it was angry and might bite. And on certain pianos that *is* the only way to get a good sound. But it's just one of many touches."

Constance Keene, of the Manhattan School of Music, is constantly surprised at how few students at the college level know the difference between producing staccato (sharply distinct) and legato (smoothly continuous) effects. She expects her students to know how to work out technical problems before they begin the "great repertoire." If they don't, she sets them to work on Czerny études, which she wants them to play "as if they were Chopin," she says. "After all, in Beethoven or Mozart—or any composer, for that matter—the scales and arpeggio passages are melodic lines." She frequently urges her students to be less tense, but not to go overboard. "If you're completely relaxed, the fingers sound mushy, like rice that sticks together."

To Leon Fleisher, of the Peabody Conservatory of Music in Baltimore, the goal of technique is not to "race around the keyboard, but to acquire the ability to reproduce what you hear in your inner ear—whether it be thunderous octaves or pianissimos. The distinction between technique and music is a false dichotomy anyway." Adele Marcus, of Juilliard, agrees. "People think that technique is playing fast and loud or fast and soft," she says. "Actually, it's how you do everything. Technique is like money. It isn't everything, but without it you can't do anything."

Many students fidget too much while they play. "They swoon," says Ania Dorfmann, who teaches at Mannes. "It's a waste of gestures." Mr. Fleisher attributes this to frustration. "They're trying to psych themselves up to play the piece," he says. "But the feelings should come out in your hands, not your body. It's also hard to hear what you're doing if you keep moving your head from side to side." He and the other teachers recommend a relatively still head and body.

One subject that vexes all teachers, because they find such ignorance about it in their students, is the use of the pedal. "It's *the* thing that reaches the listener's ears and emotions," Mr. Fleisher says. Miss Dowis agrees. "It's a very difficult art to teach," she says, "because it's an intellectual problem unrelated to when the keys go down. You must not put the loud pedal down when you play a note. In a legato passage, for instance, it produces a terrible roar. It should come before or after you strike the note."

Mr. Masselos compares the pedal to the accelerator of a car: you don't use it all the way down all the time. "You can't have a sloppy foot," Miss Dowis says. "Having a bad pedal on a piano is almost as bad as having a bad action." Mr. Masselos has some advice, incidentally, in case the pedal falls off—a disaster that most artists face at some point: "Immediately switch to Bach."

Most students have only vague notions of what the

pedals do, Miss Keene says. "They use the *una corda* [soft] pedal to play soft," she says. "But that pedal is only a mute, as on a violin. It's a color effect and no substitute for controlling the pressure you put on the keys, which is the proper way to produce a pianissimo. And the *sostenuto*! Even a student in the Van Cliburn Competition didn't know how to use it." (The *sostenuto*, or middle pedal, lifts the dampers only from the strings of the notes being played. The damper, or loud, pedal lifts all the dampers at once.) "The pedal is the soul of the instrument," Miss Keene tells her students.

Technical ability counts for nothing, however, if it's not accompanied by the student's clearly thought-out intentions for the piece he is playing. Memorizing a piece is not enough. Mr. Masselos is fond of quoting Montaigne to his students: "*Savoir par coeur n'est pas savoir*"—knowing by heart is not knowing. If a student says to Miss Marcus, "I know the notes—please tell me how it goes," she says, "I hit the ceiling. It's like reading a book and saying, 'I've read the words—what's it about?'" She quotes Vladimir Horowitz: "They always ask me, 'How did you do that?' I say it's very simple: It took me my whole life."

Students must know the context in which the music was written. Miss Keene, for instance, makes her students translate all instructions. "They have only vague ideas of Italian," she says, "and they don't translate the French at all." She also makes them research the history of the particular musical form that they are playing—for instance, Baroque dances. "Most people play Bach's partitas and suites and don't even know they're dance movements." Miss Marcus insists that her students demonstrate that they have thoroughly studied a score before allowing them to practice it. "I take tremendous pains showing them how to work," she says. "I do everything but paint pictures." Miss Marcus dislikes "lethargic" students. "I'm very compassionate," she says, "if a student falls in or out of love or is ill. So he doesn't bring in a good lesson. But if it happens every week, nothing doing."

Discipline is rarely a problem for these students, who have won out over many others to work with their teacher. In fact, they sometimes practice too much. The ideal, most teachers agree, is between four and six hours of practice a day. More is exhausting. "When you practice, you're tuning in to what the composer's musical soul strove for, and it sometimes drives you nuts," Mr. Masselos says. "You're always trying to be extra elegant and extra sensitive, and who can do that every day?"

During a lesson, discussing a piece can take more time than playing it. "At first, language can be a problem," Mr. Fleisher says. "The student may feel and hear the intangible qualities of a piece but be unable to describe them. In the end, of course, one can't depend on words, because music transcends them. I'm against this current need to pigeonhole every part of a piece—the idea that once you decide how you're going to play a passage you've got the secret. You don't. The wonderful thing about life and art is its mystery: one delves into it, finds illumination in one corner, then it goes black. One can't ever know the total truth. But the teacher can try to explain what the student is seeing, based on his own experiences of enlightenment. It's important for the teacher to remember the frustration he experienced when he was a student himself so that he can identify a student's problem and lead him to its solution, or at least to his version of it." The reward comes when the student devises his own valid solution. Mr. Masselos says he learns a great deal from his students. "You wish you could take a year off to put all that information to good use."

The most frustrating problem of all for the teachers is to find time for their own practicing. Most of them continue to give concerts, believing that it's not possible to be a good teacher without being a good performer. "Usually I go overtime with students," Miss Dowis says. "But when I'm preparing for a concert I wish they'd all get sick. You have to gather yourself back inside."

Playing a concert requires more than practice time. Personality projection is essential, and Miss Keene stresses the importance of stage deportment. "It's the first impression you make, after all," she says. "Do you fall down over the bench, or do you sit down gracefully?" She tries to impress on her students the difference between a rehearsal and a performance. "When you perform you must be a true re-creator," she says. "You must know the piece so well that you can almost improvise on the spot. It's hard to recapture the initial enthusiasm after all the drudgery. You should be *thrilled* when you perform. If we're really artists we must inspire the audience to want to be there, to leave the concert different people from the ones they were when they came in. You don't want them to think about the shopping or where they're going tomorrow. The big test is whether they'll come back and pay money again. Or even accept free tickets again."

This advice presupposes that the student will have the chance to perform. Actually the conservatory graduates who intend to perform vastly outnumber the few who will succeed. "Let's face it, not everyone can be a great concert artist," Miss Keene says. "You have to make students decide what they want to be." One common alternative is teaching. Another is to seek a career as an accompanist or to play chamber music. Or to play another kind of music altogether, as Peter Nero, one of Miss Keene's former students, chose to do. "I don't understand teachers who say, 'That student plays jazz; he shouldn't be here,'" she says. "Well, why not? Why shouldn't he have a marvelous foundation?"

After years of study, a student usually has a realistic idea of what kind of career he can expect. "Most Juilliard students are pretty down-to-earth," Mr. Masselos says. "They know that hardly any young concert pianist can make it by himself. There are thousands waiting for opportunities, and it's amazing how much talent there is." The ideal concert pianist, he says, should have these qualities: good digestion; a love of parties and of waking up early the next day; social ease; a pleasant personality; style; and an independent income that enables him not to teach. Connections should not be discounted—conductors often find work for young musicians or help to place them on a faculty.

"Chance determines careers to a great extent," says John Perry, of the University of Southern California School of Music. Although he finds little correlation between talent and success, other teachers assume that talent will out. "There's no such thing as mute talent," Jeannette Haien says. "It's pretty unmistakable," Mr. Fleisher agrees. "The student who knows it's for him won't entertain a moment's hesitation or doubt."

A student hoping to pursue a concert career must enter a competition, where he may be noticed by an important manager or, with luck, get an international performing contract. But competitions come in for a good deal of scorn from teachers. "I'm tired of them," says Miss Haien, who has judged many. "I finally have to base my decisions on seriousness of intent and endurance." She is impatient with students who devote all their time to practicing—as most competition entrants do. "They're oblivious of books, music or lovers," she says. "A real artist affirms life in his work and is inspired by dying parents and living children, by love, hate and politics. But these people just lock themselves away and mind their fingers."

The notion that competitions sift out the most important talent angers Mr. Perry. "On a stage you give," he says. "But at a competition you're judged, and you don't create art to be judged. Did Beethoven write in a certain way because he thought it would be well judged? Some of the finest playing I ever heard in the studio and in recitals *crumpled* in competition. The person who has the nerves of steel necessary to survive a competition is *not* the person who would give the best concert." He laments the years that students waste polishing one repertoire when they should be expanding it and taking risks. Nadia Reisenberg, who divides her time equally among Juilliard, Mannes, and Queens College, resents the restrictions that competitions impose. "I never let students study a piece just because some competition or a concert requires it—only if it would be good for their repertoire," she says. "If a certain style seems difficult to a student, you should give him more of it. Obviously he'll only prepare what he does best for a competition, and that can damage his career."

"I don't care if a student of mine never wins a competition," Miss Marcus claims, though she doesn't hesitate to name the ones who have. After all, as much as the student needs an important teacher as a credential, a teacher needs successful students. "But the students all make winning their goal," Miss Marcus says. "I try to make them understand that the greatest competition lies in yourself and your own standard. It takes time, and growing up, to make musicians. Performers today peter out quickly because they become robots. They're exploited too soon, and don't have the repertoire or the maturity to support a major career."

Miss Reisenberg finds it hard to attach any significance to the decision of a panel of judges. "One judge looks for dashing and brilliant playing," she says. "Another wants sensitive musicianship. There are as many opinions as there are judges." Martin Canin, at Juilliard, defends competitions for the incentive and exposure they provide every student, no matter where he is from. The possibility of a great unknown talent, however, seems dim to Mr. Fleisher. "I don't think some full-blown talent will spring from the fields of Oklahoma," he says. "With the broad diffusion of music and the way artists travel today, I don't believe there's any significant talent that some performer, conductor or manager doesn't know about."

One indisputable flaw of competitions is that there are too many. "Every little street corner has its own 'international competition,'" says Mr. Fleisher, "which diminishes the importance of all but a very few." Too many winners only mean more competition for the available positions, and teachers and performers alike wonder whether there will be any demand for pianists at all. "There's a myth today that there are vast audiences waiting for every serious young pianist," Miss Haien says, "but audiences only exist in proportion to the talent they are offered. Also, the performer is obligated to explore new scores, and as always there are few good new scores and a very small audience that wants to hear them." For all their flaws, however, few teachers can suggest an alternative to competitions, and all agree that they will long continue to initiate concert pianists.

"But there are fewer great pianists than competitions," Mr. Canin says. "Only God produces great pianists."

Pedal and pedal plate

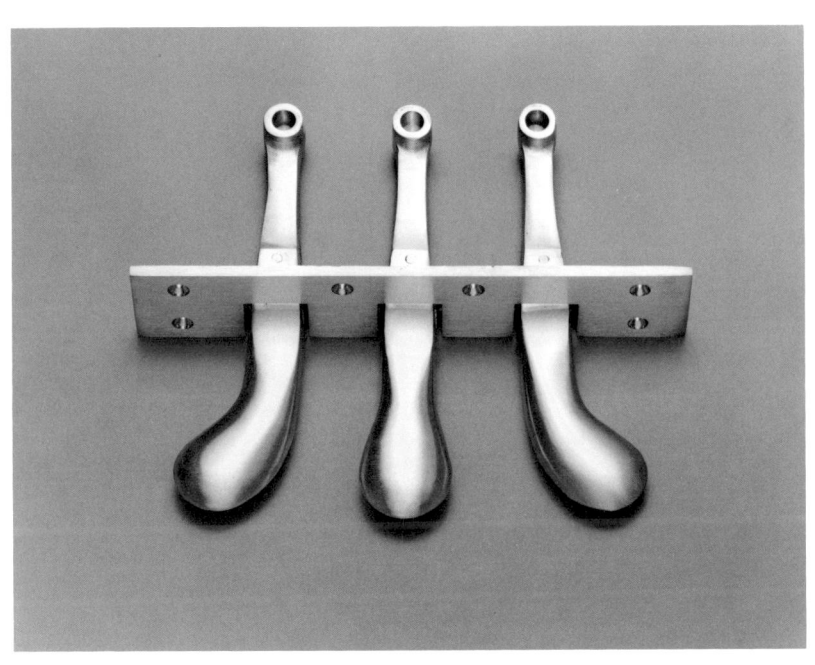

Talking About Pianos was published by Steinway & Sons
under the supervision of David W. Rubin.

Design and Art Direction by Nathan Garland
Photography by Thomas A. Brown
This book was set in Monotype Bembo
at The Stinehour Press.
It was printed by The Meriden Gravure Company
on paper made by Mohawk Paper Mills.

Editor, William Zinsser